AMNESTY MUSE

AMNESTY MUSE

poems

Doren Robbins

LOST HORSE PRESS
Sandpoint · Idaho

Cover Art: Gary Kaemmer: "The Three Graces" . 32" x 48" . Alkyd on board
Other fine paintings by Gary Kaemmer can be viewed online at *www.kaemmerart.com* or *http://gary-kaemmer.artistwebsites.com*

Author Photo: Linda Janakos

Cover & Book Design: Christine Holbert

This and other LOST HORSE PRESS titles may be viewed online at *www.losthorsepress.org*.

FIRST EDITION

ISBN 978-0-9844510-7-4

LIBRARY OF CONGRESS CATALOGING-IN-PUBLICATION DATA

Robbins, Doren.
Amnesty muse : poems / by Doren Robbins.
    p. cm.
ISBN 978-0-9844510-7-4 (alk. paper)
I. Title.
PS3568.O2229A46 2011
811'.54—dc22
                    2010052812

To Linda Janakos,
Samantha Robbins,
and to the memory of my father, Ralph Robbins

 *Let the Muses run the world*

ONE ASH LANDS

"What's up?" 1

The Song I Know My Father By 3

"Nigger Lover" 5

During The Commercial 6

Train Ride 9

My Kiev Precincts 11

Ezra Pound Left a Message on the Machine 14

Henry Miller at the Library 17

Matisse for a Minute 20

Just My Luck 21

All Wind and Dusk 23

Ritual Together 26

Night of Nine-Something 27

Virgins 29

Man with Miscarriages 30

Defending the Censorship of Picasso's *Guernica* for Colin Powell 31

The Heckle and Jeckle Show 33

Retro-Rexroth 34

Night Song 35

The Predators' Hour 37

Gulls 38

Couldn't Protect 39

Stephen Was an Ecstatic Dancer 40

My Defects Call Me Back 41

Ash Lands 43

Psychodraft 45

The Gods of Hate Were Always Human 48

TWO

THE FIRE PETAL

51 Pulled Over

53 Front to Back

55 The Scene with Monks

57 Hills, another Magic Shop

62 Tamale Place

65 Badlands and Outlands

70 Mulberry Tree

71 Buzzing Life

73 River Storm

74 The Fire Petal

75 Serenade Concoction

76 Where the Screeching Came From

77 The Weaving

79 Glass of Tea

80 Chain Open

82 Alone Together

83 The Sexiest Part

84 Their Land

85 In the Lobby

86 My Boat, My Waves

88 The Crane

89 Hummingbird

91 The Stability Key

92 Under the May star

ONE

ASH LANDS

To walk down a street in that neighborhood
and not get hassled you had to look like
you could deal with abuse—you had to
be able to look into the lowered
car's tinted window when it slowed up
to you, playing heavy bass you felt inside
your buttons, until it pulled away, because you
looked like you knew and were not surprised by
what that sound-track to a miserable time
on cheap chrome wheels was all about.
And you never let up remembering
the faces outside Wood Shop 232,
especially the one you thought was ready
to rip your skinny white ass to pieces—
and he was you found out later, but nodded
"a'right" when you said "for you, but bring it
back sharpened," and tapped each other's fists,
his holding the handed-down chisel you brought
into the shop. And you had to know and still
better be able to twenty-five years later
know again how to say in the right kind of tone,
"What's up?" And you have to say it
with your eyes looking straight but maimed
and steady with what they know from what
they have seen that any harm someone intends
for you isn't going to be justified or worth it—
and you better say it without anger—
and you better say it with your hands
outside your pockets, because you
have to show in that look that you know
the unwanted guest sits on a thorn,
so someone wanting to mess with you
senses you know it, and knows
for sure you deal with it,

because you do, and because that
is going to be
your bond.

THE SONG I KNOW MY FATHER BY

The idea of my father, fifty-two listening
to Eric Burden and the Animals' version
of "The House of the Rising Sun"
blaring out the digitalized Honda sunroof
is absurd—the radio was never on in the car—
my father was a whistler—

"Honeysuckle Rose," that Fats Waller song
of the imagined, the improbable sweet
flower, that was his melody. He almost always
whistled it while he drove—I'm not saying
he couldn't yell a child down
to the cellophane girder of himself—I'm not denying that—

the only person I ever heard call someone a *jack-off*—
"A-h-h-h, you jack-off—get your hand outta' your pants
and drive—*turn already*—for chrissakes!"—the same person first thing
found my cousin Marvin—Marvin, about an inch and a half away
from being what used to be disdainfully not even confidentially
referred to as a complete dunce—was the first cousin

gathered up in his arms when the family came together
to eat and knock political leaders while they played poker,
telling their stories about pregnancies and debt,
relating remedies to look less bald, announcing imperatives
on that very day where to find the oranges with the sweetest juice
at the lowest price—"don't forget it."

When there was a pile of money in the pot—to make a winner
we used to kiss the folded-down cards for them.
My father nodding to me, he asked Marvin,
"Kiss this card to win, I'll give you a buck, Marvin,"—
he with that smile, thirty-three years later
turned into a perplexed grin.

I think Fats Waller was into the flow so deep
he made a fantasy about sweetness
with his melody, "Honeysuckle Rose."
By that song I knew
when my father was on the pathway
between box hedges—two years after

he worked his ass off in an airplane parts factory
toward the end of the Korean War—the salesman
back from a call, usually from the middle of nowhere,
whistling out there, the father home from work
before the arm of great hair held me up
to the face with short mustache bristles

I endured like anything else
unpleasant in love.

"Honeysuckle Rose"—
I don't know what I mean to say exactly
about that song in relation to my father.
The man just whistled it.

"NIGGER LOVER"

I called this guy out, I completely lost it,
I tore into his gut, his eyes went wild he wrecked

my ear with his ringed fist I felt
I would cave in from the pain
and pissed on his mother with words—

he shifted me into a bear hug and I tried
to break his foot with my boot heel,

threw an elbow and heard something crack
in his eye socket—I didn't hate hatred I hated
sons'a' bitches like him spitting on my shirt,

then charging he tripped all the way down,
grabbing my leg and biting a spurt of blood and skin

out of my ankle, and I kicked him in the mouth
then I kicked him in the throat and he spat some
extra blood and came up on me insane with cuts on his nose

—I hugged his crotch with my knee, I had my justice
closing his tongue in blood with my forearm
when he lunged at me again drunk

with getting his ass kicked—I bent him easy
then dumped him over the rim of a lunch-court
garbage can and rolled him, when I was fifteen,

when I was with my first love from Peru,
when he said under his breath, "nigger lover,"
when he winked at her, after he said it to me.

DURING THE COMMERCIAL

I had to find a Hungarian Jew
some Ritz crackers and a compass—
reminding myself—hurrying

to zip it all back in—if I can walk through
the doorway, make it all the way back
completely into the room,

if I stay on Ogden Drive or Longwood Avenue,

if I don't go near Queen Ann Park
where the *vatos* throw bottles
at Jews,

if I don't wear a star,

if I leave
my kinky hair in the oven—

if the fan inside the refrigerator doesn't
suck me through the vent—

I'm eating somebody's chopped liver—

if I bring a little extra rye bread
for the makers of lamp shades out of
themselves made,

if I save a little paprika
to powder the broth,

if I bring
my mother's Old Gold spun filter
cigarettes and barter for some short rib
drippings to pour in their watery stew—

somebody takes and then numbers
the cigarettes,

somebody measures and then
calculates the drippings, it's not a good deal,
it's the deal without recourse or no deal at all—

if I made it through the hall from
the bathroom to the kitchen and back
to the television before leaving
the underground tunnel I dug
in the hall
in my mind
that no one entered in time—

if I returned before the commercial ended,

if I didn't forget the kosher salt,

if I didn't forget my father's Okinawa souvenir
army blanket scratching misery to touch,
scratching misery to remember it made him
sick for life—shipped overseas—

if I could steal the neighbor's car
and fill the trunk with Jews
and cover them,

if I could say, "no matter what,"

if I could say, "the stew soothed them,"
when dragging the loaded-down blanket
from the hall—

if it wasn't
an eight-year-old's dumb fantasy illusion
relief—the cigarettes—the bread—the meat

in my mind in a pot on the blanket,
the combat boots my brother bragged about
winning in a card game—

if the somber, odd,
un-Doowop-like, un-
Colgate commercial jingle-like,

all violin abscess eyes shaved starvation
corpse footage musical score

didn't return pulling through me, starting again.

Started out on the train, Eleusis to Mycenae, the goat
across from me, the rooster pecking the side
of my bag where the sausage was. "Real stud."

The old Greek stared at my beard. His lurid voice,
the bird stretching back to the basket in his arms.
Not much to say about roosters, I admire them,

their anti-Blues daybreak Orphic compulsions,
renewing ongoing sexual strut.
I raised my approving eyebrows, like I did for the goat—

something, the smell, maybe the weirdness of the dangling
throat, the intense feathers, made me sullen.
The eyes, the singer and fool Eddie Cantor had eyes

like the rooster. In that film peak of kitsch he sang
and made me sick
with his skinny mouth, then touching his finger-tips together,

lifted his eye lids back like a flea before it drinks.

I watched her eyes go like that, no way to move,
her moistened eyes—
I wanted to laugh, an old woman, I didn't laugh—I was twelve,

packed in a crowded bus—shorter and valleyed by shoulders
and backs of taller passengers—she reached, her eyes
going in, rubbed along and gripped my cock—I had the brain of

a shoe string, I had the brain of a toy bird, hard with a kind of
terror I burned on the plate of a spider. Unflexing her palm
and fingers, her eyes became clear, matter of fact, she let go,

rubbed her knuckles on her teeth, stepped down quickly,
raised the same hand to the chrome rail and got off the bus
squeezed between five or six others.

I was glad for the descendant of Satyrs showing off his two animals,
glad for the couple across the aisle, their mouths roaming
each other's faces like they were licking warm pastry syrup

out of a wrapper, warm this licking warm that.
I stared and made out my shrunken face in the chrome handle
of the window.

I was on the train to Mycenae. I'm not big on trains because of busses.
I have my feelings about roosters.
When I bragged to my twelve-year-old friends they thought

I was freaky because an old woman held it, and the way she held it,
and where—they swept me to the floor, they had their feast,
I had raw waking dreams, I marked the day.

We passed the ruins of the Great Mother Goddess of Greece
in the smog. I adjusted myself to the window, the olives
ripening out there, and the almonds with less of their skins left

to expand into, ripening out there.

MY KIEV PRECINCTS

In the closing montage
of the film *My Kiev Precincts*

the village goats trot
backward into the field

with their chopped-off heads
lowered to the ground again—

the nipples bleed in reverse,
they reattach to the mother's breasts—

the cantor's tongue
reconnects, he finishes

the prayer over wine—
the raped girl stops shaking her right leg,

the glass in her cut face
is a green bottle again,

the ladle returns to her hand
dipping the red beet broth—

the wood they boarded-over
the windows and doors

of the filled-up temple
before they torched

the filled-up temple
returns back to the table,

returns back to the cart and the door,
returns to a pickle barrel,

returns to a large puppet
with a knife in its boot

for the next time—

the re-circumcised
are de-circumcised,

the blood unsprays
from the wall—

the stomped unconscious appear
to be kissing the boot bottoms

as they arch back from the raised legs
of two killers, putting back a bottle,

unlighting a candle,
letting go of the face,

their laughter untwists
back into their mouths—

and the rooster nailed
through the eye onto a post

with the carved village name,
drops down fanning

his wings around a hen
with moist feathers

as though never interrupted,

the hen's wings toss back
the fire set on a thatched roof,

which reassembles out of the ashes,

which unburn the roof thatch,

which begins to barely vibrate

from the closer pounding

of the men,
of the horses.

EZRA POUND LEFT A MESSAGE
ON THE MACHINE

Hey this is the U.S. poet Ezra Pound. Is this the right number?
Are you a World War Two veteran or a Jew? I tried
calling before but the person that answered

wouldn't speak up. Possibly there was a bad connection, maybe
I put my fingers in some of the wrong holes. Hello? Hello?
This is Ezra Pound, in my earlier days

I spoke directly to Robert Browning, the way I wrote American English
kept up the naturalization language revolution in world poetry
our own Walt Whitman

began in 1855, continued, blended up through Langston Hughes,
out of some slave songs, Mississippi Delta, Urban Blues—*get down
Muddy Waters Chuck Berry and James Brown,*

hang it all, Joe McCarthy, I knew the Devil's Music when I heard it.

Hello, I'm calling from Italy, this is Ezra Pound, I wasn't always
a bull-shitter for Internationalist Fascism Inc.,
I wore marvelous pants cut from the felt

of a billiard table, I wrote my share of love poems, though,
in all honesty, orgasms do not last long enough.

This is Ol' Ez, if you're a Jew I'm sorry for speaking toxic waste
economic ideogram language and spitting typhoid
worm exterminator romances into the cut open part

of your peoples' organs when the German doctors conducted
their scientific experiments without anesthetics. Maybe
they were just testing? Science can't fall back.

And what are anesthetics anyway? They're only artificial aids
for denying the effects of immediate sense perception.

Students of literature who are not WWII veterans or Jews,
do not dismiss me as a miserable racist asshole
that in the process wrote an often-obscure 700-page poem,

but as someone who gives you necessary research pains
in both sides of your buttocks.
How many times do I have to tell you?—this is Ezra Pound,

aren't you listening? Are you there? Each call counts for my service.
I'm not a bubonic flea. I preferred one form of
nationalist-economic-racist-torture to the other lesser forms of

nationalist-economic-racist-torture. You probably don't know me,
I was convicted of treason, but for my crimes to the State
I was spared the hemlock of the electric chair.

I'm the poet in the crossword puzzle who emigrated to Italy
as soon as he got the chance, as soon as it was legal,
almost before they let me out

of the actual cage I was imprisoned in as a criminal propagandist.
I got out as fast as I could so I could go to the opera
where you are meant to go to the opera, and, as we say,

as fate would have it, so Allen Ginsberg
a Jew poet from the States would visit me and play the famous Beatles
rock'n'roll song "Eleanor Rigby," and, out of habit,

the Beat head smoked a cigarette of marijuana while the music played,
but I've seen poets in worse shape, and I picked up and lived with
the scent of a smoke that wasn't as sweet as all that.

Do I have the right number?
This is Ezra Pound.

Are you a World War Two veteran or a Jew?
You don't know me, part of my community service work
for aiding the Fascist enemy in World War Two was to call

20,000 U.S. taxpaying war veterans, Jews or their surviving families,
and thank them for their efforts and their sacrifices.
Your name is on my list.

Thank you for listening. Goodbye, *adios, bon jour, sayonara, gligvot,
arrivederci, clak-clak, shalom.*

HENRY MILLER AT THE LIBRARY

Met Henry Miller, I was 20, I took the bus up there,
the UCLA Powell Library.
They were celebrating his birthday. I saw him standing outside

a small crowd and went straight over—I shook his hand—I shook
what he touched—I just stood there.
He was a dried-up 80, he brimmed with a current,

he was exactly fifteen months old still wearing a dress
when Walt Whitman died.

He saw his own sphinx. I read all his novels—he answered everything.
Everything right. Everything wrong. He hadn't lost his left eye
yet, they hadn't carted his balls off yet,

he still had eleven hairs or something, he wasn't far from his cargo,
his emotional genital sweat cells under the microscope,
his microscopy, his data,

his uncensored entropy. Ponce de Leon's puddles
still splashed his cuffs.

He was going over and going over age and decomposition
with a tweezers, with a serving spoon,
with disbelief, with exhilaration, with a new love—his last writings.

I could just see him thirty-something years ago
wearing the same black laced shoes.
I could see his flashlight jutting ahead of him in the Big Sur woods,

the chorus of women laughing behind the evergreens sticky
with fir cones in the dark
in the damp heat.

I sensed his anarchist-anti-business-anti-government anti-authority
in the way he waited there unthreatening in his own existence.
I think he would've handed me

five bucks if I asked him. You can't just decide to become a person like that—
that's what he did—his body was the ground, you can't pick
your doppelganger, dreamhead double, shorter twin, non-identical identity,

nobody, better him, better him than those two.

He believed infidelity was natural—he believed that, he had to then
believe instability lying self-recriminations were natural,
possibly desirable. Maybe not.

I read all his interviews. What was he thinking? It took him
the ecstasy and all of the antonyms of ecstasy
in five marriages, it took him the un-figure-out-able

lastingness of ecstasy, it took him, it took his conundrum. His exuberance
transcended conceit; his exuberance transcended whatever
mess he was left with—

his to leave. He was the *who says you have to be subtle—exuberance
transcends subtlety*... quiet-quiet, smiling at the holes
and the shaving cuts on my face, saying,

"Time to go inside."

Powell introduced him singing on and on about his place
in literature beside Rabelais, Whitman, Lawrence,
Thoreau. I thought only Thoreau of *Civil Disobedience* belonged

in that tub. He delivered a low-key thanks to the full house,
for attending. He was halting when he spoke, he didn't believe
writers should read their work
in public—he had "repugnance for ceremonies of any kind."
After a few more words
of thanks he sat down, and things ended.

I took a leak in the UCLA bathroom. Spotless tile and bowls.
I hummed Charley Parker's "Relaxin' at Camarillo" to myself
at the urinal. Grungy, grungier,

the only word for that guy washing himself next to me.
The whole zit pit. And someone pinned him
with a Republican button. What was he doing there?

The flags are out and the bombs are dropping. For all of them

will have a ripping boil here, a tearing hemorrhoid there,
with the rest of us.
I washed my sweaty face. I gagged from whatever was coming out of
those vertical chutes.
I gave him a quarter when he asked for money for

something to eat . . . looked away from the writing on the back of his hand
then pushed through the swinging door.

At my apartment I lay down hurt, I don't mean feelings, I couldn't
locate anything.
I curled up, I still don't know what it is, what am I really?

MATISSE FOR A MINUTE

Here I am thanking
Matisse after thirty-three years,
looking at his paintings against
the hoard of compiled trash,
what a load, the padded gear
we occupy, the way we look at things,
the way we think about color. But his women
are too passive to be believed, in fact, what
am I saying? I don't trust Matisse at all,
he is so undark, unconflicted, too pure to
interest my palette. But I'm thanking
the painter for the heat of color he left.
I thank him for the red, especially
of *Le Studio Rouge,* blood-opposite red,
oven-opposite fire
of the Hallmark Card of Hitler, if it is
Hitler, "The Oven Master" himself
flaming to death in his bunker doused
with Texaco gasoline; it was Texaco
he imported until 1942; a modest
easily negotiable amount
for his bombers, his tanks, his day
in the fire, his ritual, his . . . whatever.
But Matisse, Matisse made an Eros of color,
a flood the eyes live to ride on. His color
labia opening under my lids, surging
down their dripping source, the color nest
in every one of his strokes. So not every
damned thing I think about 1914 to Gaza,
not everything is left gouged out,
necrophiled, stomped into burnt stubs,
burnt sleeves' ashes, thanks.

JUST MY LUCK

I'm reading Bulgakov again. This time: *Heart of Dog.*
That's about my speed. But what the hell is Bulgakov saying
about the system he lived under? In Bulgakov's system

the common people are dogs. Eighteen million disappeared
into the Gulag Pound—dogs, comrade, dogs.
Don't forget—they disappeared for the lowest bark, the least growl

of resistance, lack of obedience, even suspicion that one might growl,
might resist, might show her teeth,
wet the floor fearfully, not understanding the command.

Most of my dogs got out of Russia—they dug under the fences
they couldn't leap. They weren't going to see
the revolutionary redistribution of whatever rubled equivalent

of nickels and dimes, and now, seventy years later, a re-confiscation
for the worse. My dogs, the men anyway, if they could find them,
that is, were going to see the front of the front of the front lines,

or another Cossack death-squad ride-by. They used to say the Cossacks
shot from their horses with great accuracy, they could *My Lai*
a reasonably-sized Jewish village in an hour or two.

For my dogs there has simply been a fifty-five year moratorium
on pogroms. Here, anyway.
So far, that is. Not everybody's grandparents were driven enough

to get the hell out. Not a little thing. Those old-timers knew
how to run and when to run when they had to.
I bark when I feel like it. Up till now, no one has called the cops

or reported me to the Brotherhood of Aryan Shit Lovers.
And for a while I've been unbelievably lucky to keep receiving
the uncensored and therefore accurate—if not always kind—facts

about myself, so I'm not going to howl at my own reflection like
Bulgakov's dogman does. I'm not in a 1937 police state;
I'm in a 21st century semi-pseudo-quasi-partial democracy. I'm working it out

in one of its global-industrial suburbs. And while I can, while it is still
permitted, I'm goin' t'go sit outside and get me some sun,
then I'm goin' back inside and French me some fries, after that
I'm packin' one bag and drivin' down to L.A.
to meet my sugar for some tea.

ALL WIND AND DUSK

You connect again the wind Eros and Psyche ride.
You live for that wind. But Montaigne was also right

about absorbing the pleasures
of this life with anxieties of intensity,

deliberate, unswerving, and then
finding in them, when considered in detail,

little more than just wind. But what of it?
We're all wind, and the wind itself

in many ways a greater phenomenon
than anything walking here

is content with its own functions
and doesn't desire stability, or solidity,

qualities that don't belong to it.

They don't belong to us, blindness
and garbage is more like it,

and always more than we think we should get.
Lucky if you see any of it, in time.

Sometimes we see better
as a couple, even when the garbage

gets tripled or quadrupled or, or . . .

One time I thought the garbage
had no bottom. And the night I saw it

that way, ceramic dogs and robots
tried to kill me in a dream.

It mattered. It didn't matter.
In that room in the south of Crete

in the middle of eating our lunch,
I hurried to lift her

off the chair, carried her
to the pulled back bed covers,

and she opened my mouth
with her mouth,

maybe the only mouth that matters.

From the bed we saw
the waves flung backward

below hard canyon winds, violet
bougainvillea foaming

and whipping the palm of dusk.

I filled her drowning bud, all
appreciation, always

appreciation for that.
Then I had to look away

from her face so I could
stay inside of it where she

couldn't see me—muted

bougainvillea light shading

the wall and her hair, shading
the tops of her shoulders, flowing

on the sheet and our hands,
the dusk lamp flowing

through the bougainvillea petals.

RITUAL TOGETHER

I meant to ask her about a cup
we brought home from Greece.
Harvesters carrying long sheathes of wheat
in the carving that spreads from the handle,
circle the cup. And those harvesters move
with expressions of pleasure, a few
with the dream eyes of being drunk.
They celebrate because their farms are lush.
Wildly the ones in front are singing.
Maybe in that song they are thanking
in a drunken ritual together
their old goddess and her daughter
who tend the fertile ground.
It's all far off on Crete.

I thought I remembered what I meant
to ask her about it—I thought,
standing there at the sink, I remembered,
staring down into the water
of a mixing bowl where she laid her
underwear to soak out the blood.
I remembered, staring down,
what I meant to ask, but I didn't
say anything.

NIGHT OF NINE SOMETHING

Night of nine-eleven
my neighbor's orgasms brought me to the window.
And when she finished and picked up again, paused and reignited,

and then dallied, huffing beyond the wall behind my bookcase, and then
started over, roaring on her sailboat wallpaper (all of us had
sailboat wallpaper in that building), then stopped when

something that sounded like a lamp was
knocked off the dresser, and there were a few seconds of dialogue
before they began again, and he, except for what sounded like short

grunted remarks, was quiet the whole time, whatever that was about,
and they were suddenly cooing after it all, and something like
half an hour passed—I read about the losses, poisoned air, high-finance

deals between our filthy rich and the Saudi's filthy rich—then there were
whispers, a few more fits and starts, and another burst, but I didn't know
what that was about because it sounded solitary

and I thought I heard a goodbye, I heard (almost an hour before)
a car start and pull away
from her garage space directly below me—heard something

like someone running a bath, and I settled down a little from all the
excitement and tried again to read print so small I needed my
heaviest magnifying glass

to make out that Ronald Reagan's colon cancer started
with a fungus that spread from his heart.

Nine-something at work we had a few minutes of silence for the ashes
and the random parts of bodies. Black ashes they swept and swept.
The clean-up crew sucked off asbestos,

who knows what else; and the sanctions continued in Iraq, the sweatshop
scene went no place fast, wages hurried up to wait.
In the conference room we split into workshops to select volunteers
needed to escort our Arab students—a lot of black cereal before school,
the kids ate their burnt zeros, a lot of people pledged allegiance

to more fungus around the heart, and to what Bush the Second referred to
as putting a stop to "a world of madmen, uncertainty and potential
mental losses."

Night of that night, in the year of the International Rat,
and the fecalizationizers were in power like never before,
sharpening their knives

like they'd been eating with their fingers
until then, like they never had Abundance Unlimited Incorporated before,
like their businesses weren't going to make more
billions on what was destroyed and what was going to be destroyed next,
and what was going to replace the destroyed.

Nine-something. Read 'em and weep. In Redwood City.
In the Empire of Low Wages. In my hardwood room.
In the Democracy called Worms and Advertising.

VIRGINS

Hunched against the wall, ninety-one degrees, August, night—
he crawled out the window—he ran in the dark—

the two fourteen-year-olds, in the entry hall he pressed
his open mouth on the front of her thighs, her ankles,

all he could reach till her astonished mother broke them apart,
hitting them with a broom then stopping to slap the back of

her daughter's head. Still alert thinking of her sweat thick hair
sticking to her face, the fold of her lips, the vaginal throat,

the sonata soaking inside of it. He was actually figuring the chances
of whether a deer really does lie down with a virgin, as in the old

tapestries, as in the mind that made a good allegory,
in the mind awake with the animal smell, and the tenderness.

And it could only be good to be that close to a deer, to have
red and purple dahlias there for the deer to eat—aren't they

the blended color of a deer's mouth and therefore a kind of
twin growing beside the virgin's lap, where the deer lowered

its head, so, in the allegory the deer is also her lover, and there is
no truly crazy mother swinging a broom and then resting it

so she could pull her daughter's hair, start shrieking in Hungarian
and Spanish, then pleading to some god about this and this

and spitting at a deer and knocking a rubber plant over,
and sweeping dirt onto the Mexican tiles, spattering dirt inside

the rose cactus heads
and the bathing suit bottoms.

MAN WITH MISCARRIAGES

And those two, that chaos of the kidnapped weight,
those two with the sucked-out blood at the other end of themselves,
and the one who lost them, who hears their two languages
still, and plays them back

to meet them again,

and then runs the sink water louder
to lose them.

Now he knew what that voice was in April,
those were the voices he didn't know,

together in that singing rasp,

a little low, and then pausing in the night,
the just audible voice

in the live oak, the just born voice.

He missed hearing the cries in the night of them together,

he missed hearing the shuffling in the leaves of the night tree,

he missed finding in the morning
the empty eggshell still warm on the ground.

DEFENDING THE CENSORSHIP
OF PICASSO'S *GUERNICA*
FOR COLIN POWELL

We covered the tapestry of Pablo Picasso's painting, "Guernica," hanging on an outside wall of the UN in dark blue cloth unless someone inconsiderately and unpatriotically made the association that by going to war with Iraq similar events might occur; that is, the comparison, which is not there to make, is a valid comparison. The bombing efforts of the Nazis in Guernica, with the high-octane blessing of a U.S. gasoline manufacturer nearly seventy years after the fact, need not be alluded to at a press conference announcing the bombing of Iraq. The previous long distance attack on civilians is no longer the issue. Furthermore, not all bombing is the same, whereas the painting might inspire a traumatic memory for survivors or descendents of that previous "war event," and the State Department might thereby be considered patriotically disrespectful or liable for reparation.

Please keep in mind that Mr. Powell is a great general not an artist or a worker in the art field—he has only the medium of words to defend his opinions—missiles and other military forms of persuasion are not the issue. Unlike Picasso with his debatable wild images of detached body parts, a hysterical mother holding a dead child, and a shrieking horse with its forelegs blown off—Mr. Powell cannot rely on such visual appeals to emotion, his words alone must reach people's feelings about the absence of effects of the bombing not shown to people who have possibly never seen bombing other than in motion pictures or documentaries, when permitted.

Therefore, General Powell is not short-changing anyone in his effort to convey how the bombing they will not be a part of will not come about as it did in *Guernica* since there are no oppositional points of reference left uncovered to remind anyone in the first place.

It should be stressed again that Mr. Powell has only language as his medium, so any competition with the great Spanish artist Picasso, though nearly forgotten among those alive today, must be deemed unfair.

Certainly Mr. Powell must have gathered educational information from his research and with the help of his advisors determined that the impact of art on visual learners plus the confusion for the visually impaired can be permanent; so, it is easily explainable why he chose to use words and permit words only as the medium of persuasion and thereby decided it would be irrelevant to keep the painting in view.

Still, one must consider the issue of a split personality and that Mr. General Colin Powell favors the side that uses language only while encouraging the omission of visual presentation. Since General Powell brought no pictures of his own, and never at a single point did he refer to a work of painted or photographic art or photo-journalism of any kind, it in fact does make sense that *Guernica* was, so to speak, out of the picture as well as absent from the General's particular word choice examples, documentation, and general references. That is to say, General Colin Powell is by no means inconsistent.

Finally, Mr. Powell is an authority on war; this is his field, that's what his creation is all about (take, for example, his contributions in Vietnam, Grenada, The Gulf War Part One, the first slaughter in Afghanistan, to name a few). And, since he has experienced the realism of war, since he has prior maximum experience as a "hero of error," and countries that are turning away from the democratic event do not feel compelled to make every opinion available, Colin Powell tried simply and convincingly to make an ordinary case for going to war, and staying there. He does not need to view art, talk things over with a military psychiatrist, nor consult oracles to solve his problems. Television stations, the Internet, and the newspapers reported the historic event. The event was not about a debate with Mr. Picasso's impressions. In conclusion, Mr. Picasso's mural is essentially irrelevant, since he is dead anyway, and he did not die in a war where there was bombing.

THE HECKLE AND JECKLE SHOW

You remember Heckle and Jeckel? They were one person played by two birds. I don't mean Heckle was the Mr. Hyde side of Jeckel. I'm talking about a cartoon, old chap. And really, how do you figure—one spoke with a British accent and the other like a guy from Brooklyn. But everything in cartoons makes ultimate sense, Doctor Watson.

One of my lines used to be, "Retsina is my drink, plum wine is my water." Pleasure is what I meant, old bean. At one point in my twenties I lived in a cave on the Island of Crete. Some part of me still lives there. "Good riddance," many people said. I lived on Crete, I lived in a cartoon. I had to clean a lot of human crap out of that cave. That's what it took. "That's what he ought to have been doing," my Greek chorus chipped in.

I knew two birds who made smart bets at the races and it allowed them to quit their jobs. When they bet my money I lost everything, my poor John Thomas. A photo finish and we lost. I thought I was heading back to Greece, Lord Elgin. Those two birds showed up missing, my liege. My Heckle and Jeckle were filled with schemes of betrayal, they followed me into that cave, I never suspected them, their accents mixed me up, they moved so fast, constable.

Those manic cartoons were like something instinctual that went out of control, Professor Higgins. They were riddles, and you couldn't stop the violence in the riddles even if you answered them, because, in fact, they were riddles about cruelty, Sir Blair. Our Heckle and Jeckle are one black feathered bird in a Blair on a Bush. Away from the studio camera they torture people in their strong beaks, then they return to the podium with their sleeves rolled up and squawk the audience back to order.

RETRO REXROTH

Back in that kitchen the two of us cooked together a few times, sautéing
at the stove, talking on and on with a kind, fragmented lucidity, told me
I should finally marry and warned me against rich women, reminding
me to check the flame under the sauce, saying the great man Montaigne
wrote how the great man Aesop saw his Master pissing as he walked
and shouted, "What! ought we then to shit as we run . . . ?" Said I should
finally settle down, said the rest is Guernica, the rest is Witch Hunts,
your poems butchered or celebrated in the *Spermicidal Review of Books,* said
marriage is twined with inconsistencies the sacrament of loyalty alters—
the rest is chemical froth in the Western waterways, the massacre at
Wounded Knee, the massacre at Kampuchea, sweatshops as foreign aid,
massacre at the Rio Sumpul, Kronstadt, evacuation to the Camps—the
rest is manic delirium militarily, no impediment—ethics of the corrupt
and uncontrollably rich—"ought they then to murder Salvadorans while
they pray . . .?" It keeps resurfacing, relocating—Kropotkin's redemptive
visionary "All for all" common sense, a vision—and told me not to let
the sauce boil or it will get too thick . . . "I know that, I know". . . told me
I should finally marry and warned me against marriage—"Marriage,"
said Mr. Groucho Marx, "marriage is quicksand . . ."

Twenty two, and to me the big lopsided body appeared unsinkable.
Before it held the stain of elements inflaming the orange blossoms,
before it entered the steady roar, still alive, in the temple of thunder.

NIGHT SONG

Not all the little birds are sparrows and quiet at three in the morning.
I draw the one mocking bird that might never relocate. That mania,
what it's doing out there, it's no longer a type of singing, not even
mocking bird-like, but tongues of jackals wagging lament alone in the
dark, in April, in the Torrey pine. The long gibing notes build wreckage
in my head. What a head. Too much plunges through. As usual.

That's my mockingbird. That's what it does, that's what the mind
and the night want me to know, me, a man diligently plodding to my
conclusions, sick of symbolic birds, tallying what I can from my average
partial hindsight.

And foresight? You can forget about that—I'm looking at *lethargia
incurablia* struggling to set in. Still—everything works, the stalk still knows
its root, intensity is beauty, one kind of beauty, $11/16$ of a truth. I don't
mean anything anti-classical, I don't mean anything too Romantical, or
even mathematical, and neither do I reject or accept all three.

Neither do I know when they'll do something about those
hermaphrodite fish living in the rivers of Great Britain, hermaphrodite
fish that weren't hermaphrodites twenty years ago.
I read most of the signs early enough. I don't remember exactly when
I stopped drinking out of creeks and streams. On our walks through
canyons I never let my daughter or her friends touch that arsenic juice.
And it was hard to stop them. They were small and wild.
I was the burro carrying five canteens.

Probably too late for me to miss the chemical stew. They're trying to
find acceptable levels of poisoned air for the number of cancered people
per million. That's what we try for now.

Mine are the defenses of a polluted guy obsessed with intensity.
Intensity enough is all.

I make a fool of myself thinking I might live any other way.

That mockingbird out there in the post-natural wind, the one that either can't locate a mate or attract one or maybe lost one. I hope it gets lucky, or chokes on a mosquito's pizzle.

THE PREDATORS' HOUR

They worked their asses off for piano lessons, dance lessons, day care—remade that junk-hole *fixer-upper* they moved into, tried to make it work for the three of them. Nikea Drand Mazek Geogria Karakos Venus Janakosov Janakos, his second wife, did as much—ended up two years later with an empty stepdaughter's room. That came after she slept stoned with four friends in a graveyard, Eugene, Oregon, second anniversary of her mother's death—that night in the nineties, two years earlier, two people shrieking bent over a twelve-year-old girl on a couch giving her their arms so she had six hands and thirty fingers to dig out a place to cover herself. That was a night without the control of their throats—a throat actually rising inside and snapping back without need of you at all. He waited three days . . . how d'you say, how d'you say . . . carried around, carried humped in his chest three days how to tell her about her mother—he loved Emily Victoria Lang seven years. Their daughter lived in a bloody egg under the hot blossom of her chest—they gave everything. They gave everything.

That was the night his face broke. That was the night he understood the Russian roulette scenes in *The Deer Hunter* prisoner of war camp passage. That was the night he understood his brother teaching him to save every moth, let them out, lift the screen. That was the night he understood why there were so many displaced chest bones in the music of the last Klezmer musician, Leopold Klozlofski, who rushed out of the forest after burying his tortured and murdered brother, and the Russian liberators came through in their tanks, and the Jews were actually kissing the tanks, and the giant Russian captain-savior-military-genius-majesty-liberator, whomever—leaned out from the hatch cover—yelling down to them, "A sin! a sin! that you survived!"

GULLS

You stop tearing the bagel and look inside
the Marina channel tide flowing out.
You willfully ignore the sea gulls. They tore
your Emily apart. You don't apologize
for implicating them. You pour out your
little fantasy of realism—the way you have to
make up the truth to tell it. You saw enough
of what happened. You wouldn't give those gulls
a sesame seed. You saw their snapping beaks.
You saw what they did. You keep
your distance from them and their enemies
the frantic slobbering dogs tearing
through sand and water to get at them.
You know what they do to anything in their way.
You know their teeth. Your feelings are clear.
And you hate with a fist coming down the gull
that trotted forward with raised wings and
an open beak about ten-twelve yards
right along side of you. You hate the way
there's always a little jealousy mixed in
with their hunger, and the way you are
always in danger—whether you never
eat in front of them, or you hand out
what you have.

COULDN'T PROTECT

You don't see what's happening with two children and two miscarried
    children in your house
in your head that day resetting the glass pane at a window
where someone tried to break in—you didn't see the gesture didn't
notice more than the chain repeated cigarette twisted out
leaving extra ash under a thumb nail—the mind-blur, the maintenance
of it, the accomplice, you wear his belt, the intrusion, you don't sense
the interior head phone turned off. Nothing you cook tastes right,
the seeds were all skins that day. Someone about to go down
stood on your neck—you didn't feel it—something sweeping you off,
rushed static running underneath—while you pushed that
metallic blue junk heap into the driveway is when it happened—
your head was in a net, too tight of a mesh again, you didn't know
what from what all over again—like you, like this, from the get go,
crouched by a wheel in your squat shadow—come out you said
to someone you couldn't protect, come back out
with the wheel that comes off.

STEPHEN WAS AN ECSTATIC DANCER

Stephen was an ecstatic dancer until he was twenty-one and I wouldn't go
to see him dying from AIDS.
I didn't have what it takes to be there to make a salutation

for comfort to him. I could've gone there with the story
about his uncle getting into an elevator with Groucho Marx, saying,
"Stephen, listen, right off he told him, 'Groucho Marx—getting his attention—

'Groucho, I've enjoyed your humor for years.'
And what does Groucho say to him? 'So have I.'"
I could've taken the chance he wouldn't've been too drugged for his pain

to hear the joke or tolerate me sitting on a bathroom rug talking and probably
having to look away. I wouldn't go see Stephen dying of AIDS.
I know compassion levels all conflict, that wasn't it.

I knew he would be sitting in a cool bath to ease the pain in his skin,
that's the way other people told me they saw him when they went over there.
A gay man dying in his bath. I could've taken the chance

he wouldn't've been too drugged, worn-down to half the weight
of his dancer's body to recognize me reading a dance magazine
or a book to him. He was an ecstatic dancer in his career and at whatever

party we were at together. I wouldn't go see him dying from AIDS.
I should've gone. I should've looked into his eyes, held him in the water.

MY DEFECTS CALL ME BACK

Back on the telephone with my defects. They called me again just outside Ventura County where the radiator poured green chemicals on my chest and arms. And it wasn't my need for coolant that brought me back to Los Angeles, I can tell you that. Always some oversight, some lopsidedness, some offspring of my stunted perceptions . . . leading the way. By Ventura I no longer perceived accidents as accidents, but as the way I arranged every choice around what was least threatening to my weak side. So little agility.
My lopsidedness. Some neglect.

My defects called me back to tell me *they* are the real subjects. To them everything else is "conceit, *everything*—just verbal spermicide, topic after topic, right-brain hobbyism, someone working a butcher's scale so it works for him, and how long are you going to look into a tailor's mirror at what is never naked about your self?" Those fucking defects wouldn't get off the phone. And what whining interiors they have, what extremes they think are only tolerable to someone who outlasted the compulsion to live extremely.

Maybe that's all they want me to know. Or is that just another disguise— that identity of extremes, and not needing them? Maybe they're not as deep as they think they are.

There I was, facing the lifted hood again. The real subject was the radiator and the patience that at least got me to Ventura. I had to answer the phone because my defects were calling me back. *I had to answer the phone.* They blamed me for the "stains of coolant" and for the radiator that was "neglected."

"Forgetfulness," I said.

"Sabotage," they yelled back at me.

The other thing, the weak side, I think it drips here and there so I'll know by the stains not where it is, but that I haven't been near it. My defects have trained me. I fixed the leak in the mounted viscera of hoses. The hose root bled because the stalk was over-heated or worn-out from years of use. But I'm not going to say more than I have to about what happened and what I think. I really don't have the right to carry myself like someone who has lost that much.

ASH LANDS

Taking in again the restaurant broiler burnt fat smell on my skin,
charcoal under my nails—a place I worked 1973—burnt Chile
smell—remember the long dinner rush—it never leaves your head—
1973 Chileans rounded-up, corralled into a soccer stadium,
over a thousand disappeared
taking the wrong street home—Richard Nixon
was their Leopold II, Henry Kissinger was their Hermann Goring.
One of those nights with my no-sleep look after a split shift—
someone making a mountain out of another
"petty international squabble" multi-corporate mole hill,
someone riding the one tricycle wheel of what's left
of the first amendment, giving back what the road can't bear.

I'm eating eggs up next to the Billy Idol of Ash Land.
I admire his belt with cartridges, I admire his pointed metal
studded wrist band. I'm passing the salt to Ash Land Billy Idol,
that imitator, those brass knuckles hanging on a chain,
his white motorcycle boots of androgyny (though he looked
a little mean underneath his androgyny). His girl friend,
with her sleeping bag tied through back belt loops; bleached
eye brows, bleached fur steel hooped belly button
vine sprung over the folded-down copper fly snap;
fish-hook necklaces; black finger nails' contempt
for the adaptation mosquitoes
I too scorn.
I don't think they diagnose the disease
they're sick of, I don't think they believe the conflicts
will be resolved—too many global banking crews and
their graveyard, grave taste, mass grave
aphrodisiac money—too many of their private
armies fixing everyone's conflicts now.

Right from the start World War One widows lived in our four-plex,
World War Two concentration camp freak-out

survivors outside the bakery-delicatessen window.
Families disappeared in Ukrainian, Polish, Russian pogroms,
Russian Gulags and madhouses—their Stalin before Stalin,
during Stalin. Ukrainian Cossacks were their Ku Klux Klan,
Ukrainian Cossacks were their 323 year My Lai Massacre.
That neighborhood, mostly short-lived machinists, salesmen,
seamstresses and waitresses, a few teachers, a couple social workers,
the Saturday matinee pedophile with a cane.
Your historical street, your Ash Land, one to five
in every state, The Union. We comb our hair
in mirrors that return no blessings.
Nose rings hadn't happened yet, pierced lips and nipples,
head-bangers, crack-heads, teenage cutters, ten-year-old needle freaks
hadn't happened yet. It was already history—Salvatore Dali with his
Dexadrinal eyes, walking a pet aardvark onto the old Tonight Show stage
during the muted bombing of Cambodia.
I hadn't had the compassionate hallucination
of Jesus nursing a dying Muslim drag queen yet.
I hadn't experienced the actualities and phantasms
of impermanence yet. The meat hook
hanging over the 20th century
wasn't full yet.

I'm talking with Billy Idol's fist, his bracelet of steel pins,
his pit-bull smirk.

The guy with bulging plastic bags outside the coffee shop
begging on the pissed ground.

Curses against U.S.-Israeli bombing of Lebanese civilians graffiti
    the stucco wall
that will eventually, temporarily, get white-washed over.
But wash, blood wash, no wash,
it will still be there in the peoples' faces.

PSYCHODRAFT

I'm watching the Anthony Perkins of *Psycho*.
My 1968 draft board. I like the tide when it stays out,
the sea has taken enough, I said.
Please explain, he said.
I'm a Raw nut man, I said.
You speak in pure inferences, be clear about what you mean,
you are not speaking in context, he said.

Don't put your slippers on the bed, she said.
They've never been outside, I said.
Yeah but they've been on the floor
and the floor's been outside, she said.
How can the floor've been outside? I ask.
Don't start talking like you're a professor of
Germsamania or something, she said.
Everything's coming right at me, I said.
Nothing's coming at you, don't start, she said.
The uncooked side of it all is coming at me, I said.
No, it's William Randolph Hearst when he was ten
asking his mother to buy him the Louvre,
that's the whole problem in a nutshell, she said.
Grateful my watch running again for one dollar, I said.
Do you see the gene for oligarchy and murder, do you
understand the technology of soybean buttons, don't you
ever question why some have the bushy and some have
the shaved eye brows? She asked.
Everything, everything it has to be, I told her.

I'm watching the Anthony Perkins of *Psycho*.
He wants me to answer:
What is the difference between plunk and throw?
My name is Ukrainian Dorn, I said.
Oh, he answered, I am Armenian Mike.
But I thought you were Tony Perkins in Psycho.

If you are Mike, I said, I want you to know,
before you got here the general's driver
stood by the side of your chair, opened his buttons
and pissed his cat skunk pheromonal spray.
Why didn't you do something? No one's
going to get that scent out of the rug,
the upholstery, what's left of my hat, or your
ivory toothpick. You might rationalize it means
nothing more than one scent is stronger than another,
but even Argus Panoptes the mythic giant with 100 eyes
failed to protect against wild passion.
How would you describe the driver's passion?
And, why was he left alone with me?
You mean quicksand, he said, what happened to quicksand?
People really used to fear quicksand. I think I saw Victor Mature
die in quicksand. What was that movie? There was a plane crash,
I was seven years old, I think they flew back in time,
maybe it was one of the other survivors in the quicksand,
there was something about seeing that guy sink, then
seeing his hat resting safe on the quicksand when he was under.
I used to look for and watch that film, 3-4 times,
it was one of those old all-week special events
they used to have on TV. I looked for it just to see the man
die in quicksand, just to see the hat.
Ukrainian Dorn, he said, I'm sorry I exploded at you.
We forgive each other. Thanks, want a peanut?

For the last time, if I hadn't come here they would've
taken me to jail. I am Anthony Perkins of Psycho,
this happened at the draft board, I sat across from
the Anthony Perkins of Psycho. He had a frozen face,
I had a frozen face. He had black hair, mine was blond Brillo.
He would forever be prevented from seeing his frozen face,
whereas I believed I might foresee a thawing face,
or maybe not, maybe not even if it rode on a neck
of the ice floe shouting. No, our faces remained frozen,
his at attention, mine partially zip-locked.

The two Anthony's. My name isn't Norman Bates.
I never owned a motel. My parents died of Dementia.
I am unarmed.

THE GODS OF HATE WERE ALWAYS HUMAN

But it's the gods of hate I'd like to figure out.
The battery cable on the rectum—on the nipple—
the cock head, the eye lid, the usual. They could
give it a little—but they give it a lot. I'd like to say,
"They don't know chemicals in the ammunition cause
defective infant cartilage missing organs stumped limbs."
I'd like to say, "The raping wasn't an easy plan."
I'd like to figure them out. I'd like to figure out
the pleasure of making money that way, the pleasure
of authorizing the procedures. I won't.
You know the Gypsy saying, "May crows bite off their balls."
May crows bite off their balls. They won't.
Our satiric culture critic estimates when the cattle-prod
electro-shocking a demonstrator will be on
the voting pamphlet's cover—but it already happened—
without some of us noticing it happened—without
actually needing to happen. Maybe permanently happened.
I'd like to figure out the hate. The Gods of obedience
were always stronger. Who wants to read about duct tape
used for bandages on detainees' untreated wounds, who wants
to recount how the officer monotones through a megaphone
to a mostly unarmed village: "Surrender or commit suicide"?—
More than I thought. You won't figure out the hate.
What is left un-destroyed?—even the bee hives are torched
when they take out a village, the added measure
for killing crops, common pathological knee-jerk continuity.
The impulse, the plan not to torture, not to bomb, not to
suicide bomb, not to poison farmland water, not to napalm,
not to crucify, not to gang rape, not to shoot all the goats,
not to mass grave, not to pogrom —always had less power.
More necrophiles than biophiles, more Mengalas
than shmengalas. I'm not the only one who gets their victory.
I shut down the torture pictures, I turn off the poem
one of their scholars wrote to defend them.
May a catheter enter his poem.

TWO

THE FIRE PETAL

If I can just get empty
enough. The little epiphanies,
there still are epiphanies,
despite the false epiphanies,

if you can withstand them.
Pulled over in the shade, more
and more drought and heat.
Eating beside my car below a stand

of Alders, the Italian crust
in white paper wrapping,
the famous Virgin's picture
printed on it, the intense crossed

wheat sheaves yellow under
her breasts. Thirty-thousand
years later, still there for some,
for me. A pink leaf

and a whitish one under it
drew me over, a cocoon
in there, little wreckage of
attachment when it passes,

that it will pass, that cocoon life
in a camellia bush, and the
absurdity of where to
fly to when it's done

programmed in the wings,
and the filaments of the nerves,
in the delicate eyes, delicate
genitals, everything delicate

really, in them, and the rest
of us, some of us. The display
of what is beneath will come soon.
I see the little electric mask

of its face behind the already
transparent sheet, the secreting
in there, the watery-branched
eyebrows, the small flying skirt,
and the color-weave in the wings
florescent-intense for mating.

The absurdity of it, and the charm.

FRONT TO BACK

Grinding my teeth I thought about passing the off-ramp on the way
into work on a day when
everything's in sync to the hilt, nothing drags—

I wanted another day on Pacifica Point Palisade.
I used to walk up and down those cactus and rose garden lanes
for hours with Monica Karakos. Pacifica Point, Santa Monya. Maybe

she's walking there now passing the old WPA-Public Works of Art
Project Brancusi-style cut
and buffed smooth sculpture of Mother Monica, Saint Augustine's

mother, her stone ass pointed at the sea. It's the one public ass
      you can look at
without starting any trouble. Monica's backside or no Monica's backside
I was thinking about giving up another junk-ass-job

teaching technical writing at Caltika-Tech.
I was thinking about shaving my head, but not all of it. I would do it
during the holidays or the not so holidays. If I buzz my head I'll do it

after taking a bath with Monica Karakos—not
before—because I know she won't go for the new look,
there would be a short intense interview about the new look,
  and I can't chance

not getting by without our bath, the important thing is to make it
into the bath, the solace of the bath, the solace
of seeing water drip down her back, an amazing back, greater than

Monica's religious spinal cord, greater than a back or any backside by
the great Brancusi or even Henry Moore, although Henry Moore
  in particular
loved sculpting the human back, you can tell he knew the human back—

every time he made the back of a man or a woman he transcended
  anatomy.
But a lot remains unseen in every back
by Henry Moore. Maybe not being able to see his own back created
all the approximations, although he too must've lingered over and studied
his wife's back—no, everything had to come out of his own back,
he had to work from feeling it, from the concave outward to its contour.

How could he be at the back?
He had to be at the front. Where else could he be? He had to be blind.
Henry Moore was blind. No back ever looked that way.
He was a blind man.

The way he made them—all backs must've been giants to him, over-sized
  shields
protecting the flaws and frailties of his men and women.

A knife-shaped back the height of two walls.
A shoulder at the top of a one-story boulder.

THE SCENE WITH MONKS

Envy those monks
in their orange robes
walking hillsides,
shitting in a hole
and troweling it over,

shaping meditation rooms
with their hand-made hand-tools,
eating a bowl of millet
with salt or plain.

I envy one monk
finding bugs in the grain
and picking them out
patiently and placing them
in low grass shade.

A single black tail deer buck
glances over then continues grazing
in the foothill field, a flock
of chickadees with white stars
in their tail feathers

swarm into the black oak,
eating, hanging in every
possible position necessary

to get the last insect or drop
of leaf-juice. The compact birds
move with a sense of
the uncontrollable,

they move with a sense of frenzy.
And I feel close to them,

close enough, close
as I can stand it,

you can't always stand it,
the partly, then totally
defeated, frenzy.

I don't know how they get over
the sexual dream load knocking

on their rocks,
but I envy those monks

impassively chopping fire wood,

one monk in a blur
staring down

at the bark shavings

dusting one side of a wood pile.

HILLS, ANOTHER MAGIC SHOP

This time they'll say: "He tried to work it through the aisle,
They'll say: "The wash cloths caught on him, he pulled

some down, their stained fabric carried his smell,
part of his cloth, his sweat."

I restocked the dark blue with the dark blue, the red
with the red. In *Hills* fifth-rate department store,

I'm checking out the *Harley Davidson*
accessories: black leather caps, German Crosses,

leather bandannas, white skulls, rebel flags,
grim reapers. What are the *Harley* people declaring?
What is it they're supposed to want revenge for?

A motorcycle gang girl pin-up imprinted
in fluorescent paint, sits on a chopper,

her arms around an actual white hog
dressed like a *Hell's Angel*. He had a swastika.

But I never saw this outside of a magic
or motorcycle shop. Maybe I was in

a magic shop and not *Hills,* after all,
or *Hills* is a magic shop at the top

of a pyramid of sweat shops
where towels and work gloves, tank tops and

plastic containers, sun visors and
perforated insoles appear and

get bought-up without any idea
about how they appear, no idea at all,

just the magic shop making things flow
out of Indonesia, Taiwan, Tijuana

or some locked-up underground factory
in Pittsburgh, Los Angeles, San Diego—

and no idea who burns out *if they can burn out*
without fear of losing a room, maybe just

a mattress, I mean their bus money, their
bean money, after eight-ten-eleven months—

as I used to walk out, one of the lucky ones,
the years '69 to '89, walked out

with what I had left, walked away from
what I came up against.

Even though I was blowing it in the middle
of a store, sweating down my back—maybe

there's not even the consolation of some
further connection with what's hanging me up,

contacting what it is, and knowing it,
so the whole effort is its own form

of magic production, and that and
only that explains why I'm always

liquidating myself to keep going,
just as I had to maneuver with it

through all the *Harley* crap, the pinned-up
painted-on woman, the white hog's hose-bag,

forgetting then remembering the pillow case,
the broom, the ointment-prescription for my

de-cancered cheek—trying to get out of
the aisle altogether, moving past the

future owners of petrochemical shoes,
leaning over their boxes, tightening

the laces to their feet, and no idea,
none of us, who could and who couldn't

walk out, or whose lungs cracked or didn't
during production so we could cheaply

cover our toe nails and foot hair and skin.
I grazed a few things, carts carrying

detergent and hangers, sturdy beer cartons,
cough suppressants, hemorrhoid cream inserters,

rebel hats, black motorcycle vests.
I came to *Hills* for soap and a broom,

for cheap vitamins, ointment, a pillowcase—
I tried to walk with everything, tried to

fit into one of the lines inside *Hills,*
to feel right in the line, a part of the line.

And the cashier working the register
started telling me she was losing her mind,

"once and for all," she joked, but she laughed like
she wanted to run, her eyebrows were wet.

I thought it was me bringing it on,
the part of myself that feels like it has holes

chewed into it. I felt like I was in one of
those petrifying transformations

in the old myths, hardening because
in this myth instead of the wrong love

I couldn't keep from entering
the wrong aisle, and I was changing

appearance, the cashier could see it,
and I couldn't stop because

it's too much sometimes to go out
for a generic prescription

and all the rest without pulling things down.
She tried to find a slip to run my card through,

then she had to call in to check
my I.D. number on the card,

harassed, telling me she's "frazzled," couldn't
find her pen, "out of it, once and for all."

I thought I was bringing her anxiety on,
I thought she saw what was happening

through all my purchases, my appearances,
or it was her own trap catching her,

the store's traps, *Hills of Traps,* traps of rooms
where the Employees Only are produced.

I was trying to maneuver my way
out of the store.

I just wanted to get past the register,
affectionate and ridiculous consoling

the cashier even as I made it along
the rail, past the artificial lilies,

the petrochemical shower curtains,
the fruit leather, the vinyl mats.

TAMALE PLACE

I'm waiting for my breakfast Tamale in the Toltec.
The Saint Francis of restaurant flies blows on his plate,
moving his tongue from one corner of his mouth to the other.
He never lifts his hand, he watches the flies on his rice,
a compassionate strain tilting his lips, both eyebrows raised.

I don't know what happened to Francis or his descendants,

I don't know why we never fully believed in the Saint of Tolerance,

I don't know what happened to us.

In line in the Toltec with immigrant masons that work for shit.
A laborer wearing one stringy kneepad counted through his change.
Saint Roach stood on his back legs to examine the cherry peppers
nesting with hard-boiled eggs.

You get used to the plastic carnations.
You get used to the portrait of The Virgin smiling over crushed chili
and fruit flies.
You get used to the gas and lard smell coming out of the kitchen.

The descendants of Quetzalcoatl make the tamales.

And you can't deny it, even while the beatings go on at the border,
even while the homely Beluga, the whales of cancer,
once known as "The Canaries of the Sea"
wash up from their toxic ocean bath
on Saint Lawrence beach—you can't deny
the tamale-pleasure, because it's a lifetime

of picking up the version of the Blood Sacrifice you're born into,
and the Blood Sacrifice Language you use to get it down.

In the lucky pile of signs I talk with to myself I work
the same collective slang—a sort of pidgin Saint Francis,
a little pig Latin line-cook Don Quixote, the straightaway

language of my Blood Sacrifice.

In The Toltec in line in the morning, as if it were the Virgin of Guadalupe
I waited it out for all night. Lupe's the only one who could spice this meat.

I was safe in The Toltec, another lucky part of everything else
not bombed and poisoned flat, not homeless, not starved into the ground
at the end of that 2004 December. That's all.

I walked back with flour tortillas I couldn't finish—I served out of a bag
what I saved to the man who sat there in the day, everyday, all day,

the man grinded down to that spot, it was his corner in the day,
he was The Dayman, at his grass border, his fire hydrant, that spot,

his Stelazine, Prozac, Demerol, Zanax, whatever it is
he receives to finally conk out on. I could only bring

what I saved from what I couldn't eat anymore of.
I could have just been tired of it. I couldn't even look
at what was under his nails.
Handing the food over, I smiled "the goodwill smile."

In line, in The Toltec, I admired how the Virgin bends
from her heart compliantly as though moving closer

from her calendar on the wall.

And we need her closer.
As close as she can get.

But she's not coming down from anywhere.
If you asked me about her gesture I would say you're asking about

a language that is irresistible, a language that often works in every way,
because it's the language of the illusion of comfort,

of assurance—a language out of whack
with the example of goodness,

because we shouldn't need of all things a virgin
for comfort, but a different life.

The Virgin of Guadalupe caught me
in the eyes of the woman working the counter.
She gave me "a look"

because I bickered with the guy beside me
about who was next in line—

because I had forgotten how the strands of red peppers
hang their sleeves, lapping the delicious garlic strands—

because their shaved heads bow
over the 500 Mary's of needle tracks—

because the crucifixion for the meat of tamales—

because the Saint Francis of jalapeños and flies—

because the Jesus of corn meal and lard.

BADLANDS AND OUTLANDS

I.

The stroke of magenta dimming the sea hill—night was my ovum—
going west on Interstate 10. Not even Venus Janakosov knows
the ragged way I drifted out of control 1976-79—drudged
my way through the ruins of Gournia and Phaestos, badlands
of Costa Mesa, Naples, Los Angeles, Portland badlands,
badlands of St. Paul, Santa Monica, Mission Viejo.

·Heading east on 34, I had the hail visitation—higher up
snow lapped the cedars and melted or flew across the engine hood,
white slivers lit the windshield—higher up

the hide of the road was black hail, my kind of hail—

you couldn't see the fish hatchery at its port below—
it was all linked up to the hail and chain
of my visitations.

The frogs were there, I went passed the frogs,
I mistook them for crickets or was it crickets I mistook
for frogs? Frogs in that cold? Crickets? February.
I was inside the visitation, too close
to the shoulder of the road, how should I have known
which music would freeze out by then?
What was I hearing?

Janakosov was there with her fear of heights.
I was all height.

II.

Going east on 34 not across Corfu—not the lightning visitation
I saw mounting on the horizon two hours—not the *taverna* again,
not the Corfu fisherman reeking Dutch beer

and another one, a man with a stone block neck
lifted a table in his mouth and tilted swaying upright into a group
of young men dancing together, before he parted them.

And the students from Sweden went out to smoke,
whispering, staying out of the way—the ones from
England and the States, more reckless, stoned, drunker
than the rest, made a circle around him, breaking glasses
and plates with the other Greeks, urging him
to lift the table higher, stretch it up
over the height he had leveled it to,
over the point he might risk breaking,
come to the edge, tear some part of himself.

Not Corfu, not the Greek bull
charging dancing boys from Germany and France.

I'm paying my respects to his table visitation, rivaling
my black hide and white hail at 80 miles an hour—

I'm paying my respects to Corfu
and to the muse of memory and to Venus Janakosov
who is more real, Venus Janakosov coming to meet me
in the hail that leaves less of you
than crazy dogs would.

And what if I rolled my car going east on 34,
losing the connection with the curved lane, losing
Janakosov?—swing right up into the nails and teeth of hail,
even while watching her pick her way over to me
through the ice, bitching a little, calling out to me,
perspiring around her lips, crouching as though
the strength left her thighs.

And how she would hold it against me if I didn't answer,
if I decided, without talking, to lose her in the hail
I chose to grind myself up in,

waking on someone else's couch,
driving some other interstate.

III.

What if I rolled the car between Tidewater and Little Switzerland
where there's nothing but fir or birch forests,
a few people living in trailers.
And what do they do?
I never see them, not even dogs at that part of 34.
I see the tub in the side yard,
what looked like a chicken with one wing
straggling over a stack of wood,
and the discarded tires, always those.

Maybe for them it's the car-part visitation, all that's left,
everything stripped from the body of that station wagon
by the metal awning,
the wagon shell brimming with rust,
maybe a car rolled in some other visitation,
maybe the ones who've crossed the hail boundary
or the snow boundary for the last time
live out there . . .

So I drove the car into the Alsea River,
so I climbed up through a window out of the wreck,
so I stood on the roof in the water

trying to see how it swept down on me,
trying to see why it was impossible not to comply,
trying to comprehend the chaos driving into a river—

and I might've stepped back from whatever it took
to end up there,

not for all the wrong reasons—
and who doesn't to some extent suffocate themselves
in the tedium of that quest for all the exact details

to deny doing what they do
for all the wrong reasons.
Screw them.

I couldn't stand but I was going to have to stand
driving a car split in two—the water rising up
on its over-sized stalk,
I rowed in the nest it wore on its back.

IV.

Springfield Badlands,
more of the same in Santa Barbara and Cedar Rapids—

lost my center in Corvallis, Coralville, Culver City, Detroit—

lost my interior hinge pin in Florence, degutted in Florence.
Sorted through again until I understood after so many sortings,
no reprieved sorting—

constriction in Florence, the rhythm and the irritant.

Another man doesn't need Florence, doesn't need
Tidewater or Little Switzerland. Alone he reads Cavafy,
tallying, inserting, testing commemorations of some loss
with the poem he read, unconvinced—

does not need Florence, drinks brandy with his lover
of twenty-three years,

and her widowed sister neurasthenically alone
for fifteen except for her and the man
who does not need Florence

up behind her, lifting her on to the bed,
driving and driving behind her, the other sister
licking the back of his neck—So Georgio,
the loudest of Janakosov's five uncles told me
of his last eleven years, regular Thursdays, in Florence.

Slogans and painted curses on the walls of Florence,
insomnia and the tension to focus myself—not exhilaration,
not imagery, some other shore

where celebrating stops, in Florence.

What I cluttered against and within,
clanged into and decided everything from,
but not exhilaration, not imagery, I hacked into myself,
no one in Florence could do it well enough.

I am a thin cat, I am a hungry cat, I was too lean
to follow Janakosov out of Florence. The trouble with Florence.
They can't hold this over me in Florence.
Who demands such results in Florence?

And to crowd the margins almost to incomprehension
because of superstition to begin a new page
in Florence,

the beggar with stumps and the child wrapped in dirty burlap
picking up change on the steps of the Duomo of their God—the cruelty
pervasive, systematically present in Naples, London, Los Angeles,
Portland, Badlands of Florence—

renewed constriction in Florence, and the sustaining presence
of Venus Janakosov,

my attraction crested, empathic, vulgar—
momentary undermined attentions, in Florence—
the fatigue and vibrant tone,

the sunflower's hole
cragged with seeds, in Florence,

the frame without angles, in Florence.

MULBERRY TREE

Van Gogh's "The Mulberry Tree"
was our mulberry tree.
Inside the museum corridor,
in Pasadena,
in heated swirls
it bloomed and tilted toward us

out of its molten roots—
the bunched,
lighted tubes
heaped their branches—

their strands, their knotted
mulberry interiors
lit-up between us

enough, so that we
leaned.

The mulberry tree is our icon.
Her back is a dove's shoulder.

BUZZING LIFE

I blamed her for letting the hornet into the house.
I therefore blamed her for the hornet squatting
on the cheap bronze statue of my dancing Shiva.
It comes down to blaming Shiva
because he stands for eternity,
human eternity, like everybody's gods.
And I had to blame eternity—
all guarantees are for suckers.

How many times have I had to say it?—
nothing makes up for the missed life.
This attraction to Shiva: his nineteen arms
that are multiplicationizations
for the emotions of embracing.
That just can't be true.
So I blamed the Phoenix,
Shiva is a Phoenix-like god,
he dances the world into creation
after he tramples it into trash—
or is it trash he tramples into dust—
or is it depleted uranium he finally can not
dance on top of or trample into anything
that doesn't remain toxic, and this fact
accounts for his missing arm?
I always wondered what happened
to that arm. What is the missing arm
of a god going to symbolize now?
He's made the dance for about
the seven hundredth time.
Not much of the missed life for him.

We get as much of the
 missed life as necessary,
some get a hornet now and then.

That feeding-buzzing-annoying-stinging life.
I know what I know about that life
bound up in a few complicated facts,
possibly one or two facts indecisively
clarifying that it might be a contradiction
or otherwise, or even hilarious
or otherwise, to be here.

I let the heavy brass Shiva someone gave as a gift
stand below a line of my books, though he's more
of an ornament than a support
because at one end a scrap
of six-by-twelve rough hewn redwood
from the front porch I built, and a garden brick
he stands beside at the other end,
hold up the heavy board on their arms.

RIVER STORM

He saw the pet cicada, he saw the orphan, that's what they called each other—she buried the doll with poor eyes, she buried her in a coat—"Which coat?" he asked. "A good coat? An outgrown coat? A coat doesn't just grow out of one of your flower boxes."—"Enough that I buried the doll," she said. Saw her looking down the rope-knot entangled bridge chopped-up floor escalator path narrow runway ramp, no way holding more than one, at least not more than one of them. Saw the face of the woman that came in and out of his dreams over 25 years, recognized her, couldn't get over who she was, lost her smell, lost the connection—"not a problem," he said to himself. He didn't know how much saying that would cost him, and he said it a lot, "not a problem." The rail was a kite string, the river water carried whole trees, sections of composition tiled roofs—saw the fuselage of an airplane, saw horses treading wildly for the water to hold them up, to run them toward a meadow—saw a moaning bull carried off in the current—saw her look away from the water rushing down the surge and close her eyes, pressing his face deeper where he had already kneeled down between her knees, the heaviest startling current he ever whispered his mouth up to—uprooted oak roots pressed under the bridge, oak trunks arched from the river flood re-submerged, tilting back up the root legs, horses panting alongside of them—saw the stringy part of the roots, saw his legs and hers dance wrapped in them—saw the cicada, saw the orphan.

THE FIRE PETAL

The hummingbird tilting back
flowing juice up where
the honeysuckle overlaps

the Fire Blossoms—
tilted as the petals
shifted and leaked back

a renewal to the long beak
and the stem of air
supporting the tiny breast.

The camellias overflowing
the window, a repetition
of the unique, sipped from

that fourteenth year starting
together. That vibrating
up around the Fire Blossoms,

that Rufus T. Hummingbird,
the sparkling violet ear,
and that juice, no the beak

lathered with juice, no,
that dampening all the way back

to the face and the rigid
feathers' roots

and the blossom edge still lapping it

was what I wanted to see
our skin reflected in,

the Fire Petal lifting us.

SERENADE CONCOCTION

Yet "the lightening is a yellow fork from tables in the sky" Emily
Dickinson reminded her enough to collate the material into a file of
interpretations overcrowding the other file on the infallibility inherent
in metaphors, and she remembered he first dog-eared the page for her
where the Dickinson image appears two lines from the bottom (in
his copy), and she never considered this declaration from Dickinson
before, how the utensil, the eating, the yellow, the fork, the lightening
connect tables, the face and the bottom of the body and eating to a place
the lightening dropped from—it allowed her to see a Pleiades of his
hands, she saw the Wine Star, she couldn't describe the arrangement,
she'd get it all wrong, she wasn't suffering from a type of information
asymmetry, she simply lacked the heave of words the tone relies on, so
he would have to trust her.

WHERE THE SCREECHING CAME FROM

I slapped a winged termite off my chest—let it
go to hell with the mosquitoes and the scorpions.
I cursed it to myself, cursed it away
from my house, maybe I also cursed
the seesaw complexities of marriage
in a dry cycle, in my shawl
of seeds grown rough, in the shades
of their depth opening, unchanged.
And it was eating me, and my fantasies
started to split me again, after I thought
they stopped when I hit 50—or was that
the lesson of 50 when I hit 50?
Stretched out under the hood
of the car, holding a stethoscope
with a long metal proboscis
on the end, placing it on
the generator, the water-pump,
the alternator, trying to find
where the screeching came from.
And then the work and the great expense
to fix it, and later, possibly
to fix it again. Was it all the training
and work as a carpenter, a mechanic,
the discipline of attention that drew
my senses directly to things
that had to be fixed?
And what about that split
that drew me the other way?
Whatever it is: the dog chases
what sticks to his tail.

THE WEAVING

July was always the month for me.
I cling to July,

there are no doubts about July.

I feel human enough and animal enough
in July.

I identify with those harvests flying
just above the rock walls,

then bursting from themselves into the ground,
into each other.

I'm talking about a plain garden with apricots
and lemons,

where the cicadas play in the sage but never show
their watery guitars.

And what is that harvest all about?
Their music is a harvest, an overflowing harvest,

whether those musicians and their instruments
are visible, or not.

I'm saying I have everything in July. I'm saying
that July is the birth of it. July to July,

a repetition
of harvests.

July, the spiders born in the camellias.
July, the hummingbird and the olive—

that's Venus Janakos' hummingbird
asleep in her lap,

that's Venus Janakos' olive,
the one with the breast inside of it.

This is what my sister stitched
to the weaving inside her brother's head.

Where the television stood. Pinewood lines grained the tea glass bottom.
He passed a shirt sleeve through the steamed beads. Where they lived
in '85 he kept a notebook with musicians and a dancer painted on the
cover. The dancer stood by a window with arms raised. The guitar
player needed the sun, you can feel it when you need the sun, even when
someone else needs the sun. If you're close enough, if you're porous
enough. It was the Television he used to watch with his daughter had
been stolen—and the silverware, everything but one Betamax cassette
left upright in the cabinet box, not much else, not much else to take.

The long-haired man looked at the bald recluse on the Yogi Tea box
sipping down his broth. He drank from a wooden bowl not a glass. He
didn't think a television would make him curious, he thought a television
would make him run, pulling on his cheeks. Bald Yogi wears nothing but
a robe, it's all steam and ashes around the trees, not all of it incense
ashes, not all of it the steam of boiling water, not entirely a recluse on a
box. He shared the fennel seed essence with him. It's communal in an
abstract way. It wasn't taken for granted.

The dancer's arms arc over her head. There's too much black in one eye,
her face is a moist hill, the painting was dated four holocausts ago, five
neighborhoods ago. The TV was a Panasonic, she didn't understand
why it was gone, it showed the classic fairy tales from a black box, she
learned to never go into the wrong woods twice. He had one daughter,
the pigs from elsewhere hadn't broken in yet. Five neighborhoods ago
he could still fantasize while he dreamed, he could calculate in waves, it
was a discipline, there was a theft, it had no replacement.

CHAIN OPEN

He was touching a mountain behind the wall again.
There were a couple of irises here and there, not a garden,
too communal, that's over. There was a crushed balance
this time, part of the mountain, part of the meadow,
part of the condition now. Plover Dune State Park,
the plover in the first place, the memory at all,
the climb to the nesting area along fir bough rungs,
all the way up the dune hill, the prohibited collapsible
dune hill, for its own reason, the danger for its own sake,
some strange determined sake. That the plover up top
lifted its wing, that it must've had another plover
growing inside, that the bulk was there,
the bulk that is precious. Up there a chain opened
in the sand dune grass—sharp light slanted off
permitting an opening, an unraveling
is what I mean, everybody wants to see some chain
open—purple chrome furnace rhododendron unraveling
August velvet grass light is what I mean. I'll never forget it,
1:33 PM, man I wrote it down, 1999.
At the rail of the fishing boat, a man, it was him,
about to lift his voice, it would be in a raw tone,
beside a woman that looked like his first sister
might have, forty-seven-something had she lived,
had she made it past the surge of parasites that fed
from her liver, from her white blood cell count, from
the growth inside the shrunken cloth of her dress.
A twenty-eight year old man stretched in a mental angle,
absorbing the Aegean Sea, for his own determined sake,
that angle they anchored, envying, not envying, the leap,
the arc, the dolphins, the trailing, the passenger garbage,
the water, the propellered waste, the memory at all,
the dolphins in the first place, you could see them flash
in the buffed side of the metal rail, in the shred
cerulean-turquoise meadow where they fed,

in his sister's thick lenses, his watery mind
in the first place, in the bulk remains,
in the comparable déjà vu,
his inference, his voltage, his transit.

ALONE TOGETHER

I need to know the name of that bird
and find out who it is making
such music I never heard before.
I'd have a start if I could see
a wing or a tail or something
but it stays hidden away
in the crowded oak leaves,
a stone with a pit wrapped inside
of it, a lifted voice inside the pit,
a made-up world. I come back
from the window, partly awake,
the bird still going, my wife's heel
resting against my shin, the bird's
voice out there singing to me about
the birth canal she let me feed from,
the breathing gill she held me inside of.

THE SEXIEST PART

The sexiest part is the way she clipped a two-year-old's finger nails
with patience.

The sexiest part is the way she read every night to
our abandoned three-year-old nephew,
and when he finally slept she made actual plans
either to adopt or abduct him,

because his young mother was cruel and didn't care that she was.

The sexiest part—that she still took her step-niece and step-daughter
for school notebooks and pencils, took them
to the Natural History Museum and to the park with the struggling
tire-swing,
and to see the Mermaid movie and all that, although, almost

everyone in the family
tried to divide us for five years.

Our life together is my fetish, my connection, my lucky fit.

The sexiest part is the unpredictable switch in her stance, which I relate
to a mare in heat I saw once
when they led a stallion around the other side of a corral, until later.

The sexiest part is that she is not "sexy," she is mild in a way that protects
the exotic aura about her.

The sexiest part is when my face washes out and her face
washes over it, and we rest on the side of her hair.

The sexiest part is the powerless magic of not parting,
but magic nonetheless.

THEIR LAND

They went into the butterfly pavilion,
buckeyes and wood whites, southern festoons,
hermit stars—and fritillaries: spotted fritillary,
pearl-bordered fritillary, marbled fritillary, queen
of the commune fritillary, high brown transcendental
fritillary, Noah in the tree fritillary—

mostly four and five-year-olds in T-shirts,
Butterfly Pavilion red, bent beside red sage, red admirals,
brick-red underside forewings violet cardinals, silky Afros,
California Pantagruels, white clown admirals, Hungarian harlequin
gliders, among peacock maenads, one landing on my caramel corn,
one sipping spilled juice from a wheelchair foot-rest—

orange tips and bath whites, tortoiseshell colossus, green-veined
white, a purple hair streak and white-letter hairstreak, labian scarf
indigos, scarce copper mint, an Adonis blue touched a wing
to my wife's hair braid, on a ketchup smear in a boy's palm
another breathed down
on a wild thread—

broad inflamed Sapphos and utopian brimstones,
purple resisters, inaccurate names, floating bursts,
color powder, sensory spice-brush swallowtails—
in their land, their pavilion, theirs.

Ate a bag of Rosa plums walking the two miles to a movie with his
    laid-off uncle.
Most of them were sweet, most of the sweet ones better than the last.
"You better touch this one for luck," he said, squinting after downing
    a bad plum.
Too late now to ask if he remembered what looked like a three-year old
    in the lobby,
with her mother bent low saying through clenched teeth,
"I'll bust your spirit if it's the last thing I do."
Not only that would come to break, he knew.

Started to gnaw and bend, crying against one raw thumb, pouring
    her face
at the stroller metal bar.
He jumped in on someone tormenting a child once and heard
    a "keep out of it you"
that froze him—he walked off, disconnecting, sipping around
    the coffee cup rim.

The lobby walls stood out—the guy that stroked on the texture had
    to be overworked
or a slob—anyone that knows the skill could not walk away satisfied.
The lumps and cracks, the mutilated stroller intensity the dimness
    held low.
He spat down a plum stone in his palm, glowering beside
the gingham print sleeve on the stroller handle bar the lobby
    light showed.
"That shade, that shade, I hate to know."

MY BOAT, MY WAVES

I hook on the boat,
my medallion from Crete,
a never-replaced chain
holds it through the loop.

I wear the necklace
with a boat to remember
what happened when I made
the stops I shouldn't have,

though mostly it has been
a life throughout I never
had to say, "should've
sailed when the sailing

was good." I wear the medallion
to remember the storm
between Mikanos and Crete
that tipped the Cretan fishing boat

with such force I thought
it wouldn't recover.
I set out to keep in mind
the boat moving

around my chest hair,
my waves, and the storm
you can't see coming,
and the water where
some fishermen learn
not to go, that place
their wives dread.

I wear the necklace for protection,
I wear it to remind me
that the one who gave it to me,
reaching up, hooking it together,

found it on Crete
in a shop in Agio Nickolaus
called Big Cheap Store,
where, in fact, nothing

was cheap, and mostly
there was only one
of everything for sale,
and the bartering

wasn't easy,
but it was done.

THE CRANE

It all came down to a crane I saw
flow into blurring dusk and shallow water.
It didn't notice me stopped there a couple of
row-boat lengths away, chewing a Tuscany loaf,
the best I could find and my teeth endure.
The poems gathered in my mind, two or three
that were no good, so I quit. Imagination, imagination,
I'm just one of its metamorphic dolls.
Walking, tolerated by a crane hunting shallows.
Really, I don't give a damn about poetry—first,
her body more than my ink, then the wave curling
on one side to form a pipe, before rising up curved
like a woman's hip, the wave releasing like
a woman's lower back, arched. First, her body.
I could barely make out the two anchored boats
that weren't there the day before,
and the long throat feeding itself in the night.
I dropped my hand to adjust the twist inside my pants.
Who was there but a bird turning its beak, a bird aware
of my heavy clothes rustling when I walked?
The crane in the dark. The two of us.

HUMMINGBIRD

Fluttering dust from his chest feathers, I saw
the shore of white breast trim,

I saw the iridescent plum

above the white barbs.
That's what he flashed

out of apricot leaves when he aimed

his beak at two scrub jays
coming into the yard.

I think the motor sound of his wings
and his flying speed made them streak back
to the telephone wire. No fight
in those confused jays.

He likes the same apricot branch every time.
He comes here for the fire blossoms, a kind of
red honeysuckle, the juice he can't

live without, the color origin that marks him
between his heart and his throat.

Sometimes his mate flies after him
and they disappear way up
into the secreting pine.

He returns alone.

Must be he comes here to rest.
He works long hours for his abundance
and then just burns it up

flying with her, flying
into the fire blossom and back.

Bursting from his branch, he dipped all the way in,
the iridescent throat wet with honeysuckle juice,

his wings so wild with motion
the untouched red blossoms
float backward while he's there.

Sprained every one of his fingers but the left middle finger [he lifts the finger when reading aloud], and the left eye in the morning, blood-filled. You'd think that fall the worst fall, the stud-wall, that second story they framed tight (they thought it was tight) started going over. What you do is cling till you get within ten feet, then jump for it like the lead carpenter, his ride every morning, the other twin, told them to do if it ever happened like that. His ride in the meantime of those years broke half his right buttock from the jump, all fingers intact but one [lifts the right middle finger].

Rather've ended reuninjured still juvenated understanding the true fact supported by the tall-tale. Really, there's nothing but the tall-tale. Rather've looked for the stability key in the two-hundred twenty-two feet of microfilm, when there weren't monitor screens with leashed mice guiding them, when there was only microfilm and he sought the key of stability studying the cultural anthropology of toy ice. Way up north he stood by those ice dolls, he still envied the hands that cut and shaped frozen unmarked blocks into wolf and seal faces with children's bodies or children's faces with braided hair shawling harp seal shoulders.

His daughter and a friend knocked on the window telling him they found a dead goldfinch. Where did you find it? On the ground after the stair. Let's bury it, he said. Carried in her palm the tiny tilted upward rolling woods' contralto elegy beak. Laid the goldfinch in a small crate they saved from packaged handmade soap. They had it ready, they padded leaves to the rim of his wings, swaddled the goldfinch in fir twigs and wild oat. Buried him in the side yard, down from the blossoming tangerines. The breast feathers over the heart and lungs vibrant at the end of vibrancy, the breast of a flying singer, his fragrance caught the ground.

UNDER THE MAY STAR

She brought the two shells, I called them "The Two Apples."

She called them "The Anniversaries," I called them "Our Wooden Plates."

When all qualities dissipate, the plural intensity.

Her feet make erotic shadows, the May star notates the ground,

the metaphor of our gravity.

The female version of my hand next to the other version.

The convection I felt, her heat brought it to me. The May star,
    the apples and plates,

the tree of cocoons, the lower shadow of her dress, the stoned bees,
    and at night

the watermelon moths out of their minds from what they sip
    and rub in the bottle-brush.

Whatever-it-is open in my mind louvered, drumming, roiling.
    The lower rhythm raised,

of the rhythm inclination, the unrelated rhythm, without the prior rhythm,
    the renewed,

of rhythm, of being planted, of the feeling of the rhythm of being planted.

ACKNOWLEDGMENTS

Abalonemoon.com: "Virgins" and "The Sexiest Part"

Allchildrenofgaia.org: "The Weaving"

Blood Lotus/bloodlotus.com: "Tamale Place" and "The Gods of Hate were Always Human"

Cimarron Review: "My Kiev Precincts" and "'Nigger Lover'"

Ekleksographia: "The Heckle and Jeckel Show" and "Stephen Was an Ecstatic Dancer"

Indiana Review: Honorable Mention Award: "Gulls"

Monterey Poetry Review: "What's up?"

North Dakota Quarterly: "Fire Petal" and "The Weaving"

Onthebus: "Train Ride"

Ourtruths.org: Abortion Represented in Popular Culture: "Man with Miscarriages" appeared as "Man with
    Miscarriages and Abortions"

Paterson Literary Review: Allen Ginsberg Prize, Editor's Choice: "The Song I Know My Father by" and
    "Just my Luck" (2005, 2006)

Pedestal.com: "Night of Nine-Something" and "Ezra Pound Left a Message on the Machine"

pemmican.com: "Ash Lands"

Philadelphia Poets: "Pulled Over" and "Where the Screeching Came From"

Poetry Magazine.com: "Numbered Events" and "Matisse for a Minute"

Poetry International: "Predator's Hour"

Solo Novo: "Stephen was an Ecstatic Dancer" and "Tamale Place"

10X3: "Virgins," "Couldn't Protect," and "The Gods Of Hate Were Always Human"

Third Rail Journal: "Retro Rexroth"

ThirdRail.com: "During the Commercial"

Willow Springs: "Henry Miller at the Library" and "Front to Back"

"Just My Luck," "My Defects Call Me Back" and "Night Song" appear in *Bear Flag Republic: California
    Prose Poem Anthology,* Greenhouse Review Press, Alcatraz Editions, 2008.

"Night of Nine-Something" was published in *Eating the Pure Light: Homage to Thomas McGrath,* Backwaters
    Press, 2008.

"Hills, Another Magic Shop" appeared in the chapbook, *Two Poems,* Rabble-A Press, 1994.

"Badlands and Outlands" appeared in the chapbook *Double Muse,* Rabble-A Press, 1998.

"The Gods of Hate Were Always Human" appears in the anti-war anthology, *Against Agamemnon,*
    Waterwood Press, 2009.

"My Kiev Precincts" and "The Gods of Hate Were Always Human" have been accepted for publication
    in the anthology, *Before We Have Nowhere to Stand: Israel/Palestine Poets Speak Out Against the Struggle,* Poets
    Responding Press.

Grateful thanks to Christopher Howell, Christine Holbert, Linda Janakos, and Adrienne
Rich for suggested revisions and clear-minded edits that improved the quality of the
overall selection in *Amnesty Muse.* I also want to acknowledge Brent Schaffer and Jaime
Wood at *Willow Springs* for their close reading and editing of "Tamale Place" and "Front to
Back," respectively.